Beginning Reading
for Older Students

30 Reproducible High-Interest/Emergent-Skills Stories
for the Classroom and the Home

by
Gloria Lapin

**Illustrated by
Karl Alstaetter, Mike Fink, Buck Jones,
Dave McPeek, and Ron Zeillinger**

Good Apple
An imprint of Carson-Dellosa Publishing LLC
Greensboro, North Carolina

Author: Gloria Lapin
Editors: Kathleen Hex, Kristin Eclov, Todd Sharp
Cover Artist: Karl Alstaetter

Good Apple
An imprint of Carson-Dellosa Publishing LLC
PO Box 35665
Greensboro, NC 27425 USA

Printed in the USA • All rights reserved.
8 9 10 11 GLO 13 12 11 10

ISBN 978-0-76820-661-6
060107784

Table of Contents

Introduction

This book was written to help older novice students learn to read English. It contains 30 reproducible little stories that incorporate emergent reading skills with high-interest content. This book will help older students who are learning to read English as a second language as well as those who had difficulty learning to read in the primary grades. It is a supplementary tool that complements any reading program and can be used in the classroom or at home. Although the little books have been written at a beginning reading level, their story content is designed for older readers.

Beginning Reading for Older Students introduces and reinforces all 220 Dolch words (see Dolch Word List on page 73). Dolch words are the 220 most frequently used words in books children read in the primary grades. Many of the words must be learned as sight words since they cannot be sounded out and therefore do not follow any decoding rules.

The individual little books are systematically constructed to provide the sight vocabulary in a controlled fashion. Each story uses the previously presented words and introduces a number of new words. Students are encouraged to use the context clues and picture clues in each story as a guide to help them read the text. Frequent repetition reinforces learning and fosters success in the reading process.

How to Assemble the Little Books

This book is divided into two different formats. In the first part, students will create their own eight-page readers. In the second, they will create individual two-page comic books.

Part I

Each story is easily assembled into a small, eight-page booklet. Prepare a two-sided photocopy of each book. Cut the sheet in half along the dotted lines. Fold the sections in half and slip one section inside the other so that the page numbers in the little book appear in sequential order. Staple the book along the fold. It's now ready to use.

Part II

The second format is to give the readers variety. Each story should be photocopied on the front and back of a single sheet of paper. The comic book story is then ready for use. There is no need for cutting and stapling.

Master Vocabulary List

The master vocabulary list (see pages 5 and 6) contains the words as they are introduced in each story. Once the words have been initially presented, they will reappear in the following stories. You may choose to present the new words before reading the story or to direct attention to them as they appear in the text. Reproducible word cards for the master vocabulary list are included on pages 74–80 for additional review. Encourage students to develop skill in figuring out new words by accessing prior knowledge and using context and picture clues.

Other Activities

Comprehension questions (see pages 69–72) can be used after each story is read. These questions can initiate discussion about the text of each book in order to assess the readers' understanding of the story.

The little book topics can be used to further language development. Discussion of a story topic, whether a televised baseball game or a trip to the grocery store, offers the opportunity to enrich vocabulary and enhance oral language development.

The little books can also double as story starters. Students can write sentences or other stories related to the reading material.

Master Vocabulary List

Book 1
what
do
you
see
I
a
TV
on
man
ball
hit

Book 2
box
in
the
is
no
not
cake

Book 3
where
here
can
bat

Book 4
milk
bread
fruit
money

Book 5
look
at
this
too
little
take
that
off
try
big
good

Book 6
looking
like
want
to
it
buy
one
am
me

Book 7
have
come
new
did
yes
for
ride
get
when

Book 8
hair
long
cut
your
sit
make
pretty
now
got
looks
will

Book 9
name
Dan
Hale
date
of
birth
age
height
feet
inches
weight
pounds
address
hill
street
telephone
number

Book 10
why
sad
something
eat
that
thank

Book 11
let's
out
put
how
we
they
cook
things

Book 12
keys
cannot
find
help
know
are

Book 13
well
much
age
walk
up
first
again
let

Book 14
show
funny
may
would
open
think

Book 15
read
sleep
laugh
before
so
book

Book 16
them
play
he
run
fast
him
jump

Book 17
work
must
always
about
some
cold
drink
tell
again

Book 18

bus
downtown
goes
stop
from
then
soon

Book 19

hello
Pat
Kim
who
saw
please
there
said
say
what's
all
Sam

Book 20

found
by
books
or
comes
two
colors
blue
green
which
should
both

Book 21

today
pay
but
together
because
use
carry
better
these
those
many
done

Book 22

nothing
clean
wash
going
laundromat
anything
water
hot
things
warm
Jane
doing
after
home
her

Book 23

was
just
with
don't
she
went
could
does
live
around
lives
were
looked
call

Book 24

wish
had
garden
grow
every
day
has
been
his
came
keep
takes
own
likes

Book 25

sitting
thinking
draw
start
pick
give
full
eight
only
seven
gave
orange
red
yellow
brown
black
white
right

Book 26

anywhere
somewhere
far
away
ask
us
fun
three
shall
once
hurt

Book 27

kind
old
small
five
six
very
write
best
light
four
its
wheels
into
pull
an

Book 28

our
from
fly
as
bring
round
on
plate
Mr. Jake

Book 29

ran
under
sing
their
Jack
ten
everything
everyone
birthday
surprise
coming

Book 30

job
bookstore
need

I see a man on TV hit a ball.

8

What Do I See on TV?

1

I see a man on TV.

6

What do I see?

3

7

What do you see?

2

I see a ball on TV.

7

I see a TV.

4

What do you see on TV?

5

No, a TV is not in the box.
A cake is in the box.

8

In the Box

1

No, a ball is not in the box.

6

9

I see a box.

3

© Carson-Dellosa

Do you see what I see?

2

Is a TV in the box?

7

What is in the box?

4

Is a ball in the box?

5

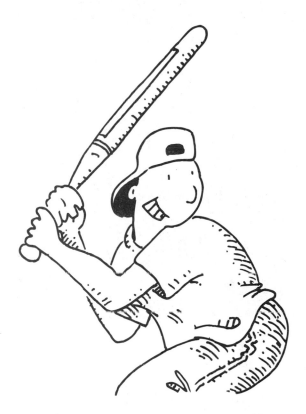

The bat can hit the ball.

8

BOOK 3

A Bat and Ball

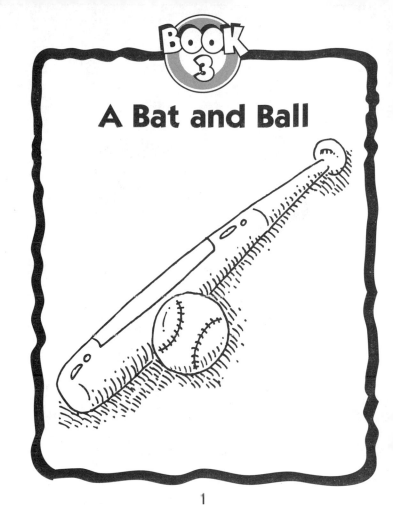

1

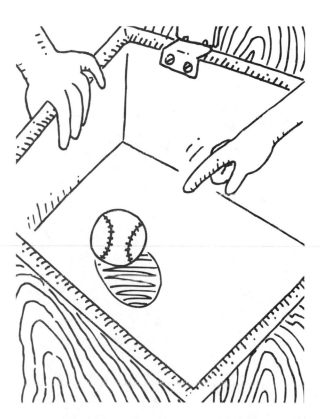

The ball is in the box.

6

Is the ball here? No, the ball is not here.

3

11

Where is the ball?

2

Here is the ball. Here is the bat.

7

Is the ball here? No, the ball is not here.

4

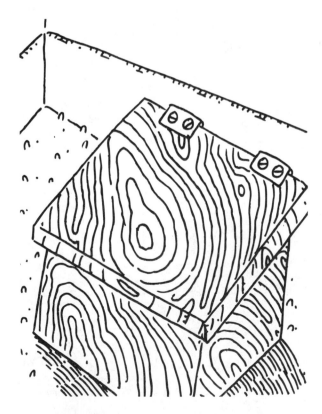

Is the ball in the box?

5

Here is the milk. Here is
the bread. Here is the fruit.
Where is my money?

8

Shopping

1

Where is the fruit?

6

Here is the milk.

3

Where is the milk?

2

Here is the fruit.

7

Where is the bread?

4

Here is the bread.

5

Look at you. That is good. You look good.

8

BOOK 5

Too Little, Too Big

1

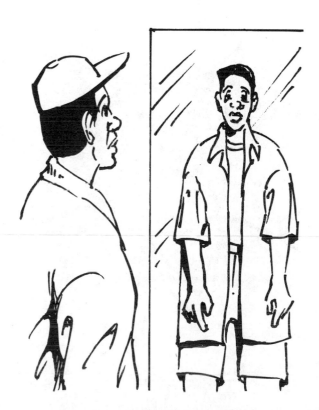

I see this is too big.

6

I see this is too little.

3

15

Look at you. What do you see?

2

Take that off. Try this on.

7

Take that off. Try this on.

4

Look at you. What do you see?

5

I look good in it. I want to
buy it.

8

BOOK 6

I Like That

1

Here is one. This one is good
looking. Try this one.

6

I like that. I want to try it. I
want to buy it.

3

Look at that.
That is good looking.

2

This is good. It is not too big.
It is not too little.

7

Look at you. You are too little.
This is too big. Do not buy it.
Try this one.

4

Look at me. I am too big. This
one is too little. I do not want
to buy it.

5

This is where you can buy one.
You can buy a new
one here.

8

Come for a Ride

1

I will get in. I like this.
I like to ride.

6

Is that new?
When did you buy it?

3

Look what I have. Come see
what I have.

2

I like this. I want to
buy one, too.

7

Yes, this is new. Can you come
for a ride? I want you to come
for a ride.

4

Yes, I can come for a ride. I
want to come for a ride.

5

I like my hair. It is pretty. You did make it look pretty.

8

A Haircut

1

Look at your hair. It is not long now. I cut it.

6

I will get it cut. I do not want it this long.

3

21

Look at my hair. My hair is
too long.

2

Look at your hair. You got a
haircut. It looks pretty.

7

Will you cut my hair?
It is too long.
I do not want it this long.

4

Sit here. I will cut your hair. I
will make it pretty.

5

Name _____
Date of birth _____ Age ____
Height _____ Weight _____
Address _____
_____
Telephone number _____

8

BOOK 9

What Is Your Name?

1

What is your address? My address is 501 Hill Street.

6

What is your date of birth? My date of birth is May 12. What is your age? I am 27.

3

What is your name? My name
is Dan Hale.

2

What is your telephone number? My telephone number is
(404) 555-3679.

7

What is your height? My
height is 5 feet 10 inches.

4

What is your weight? My
weight is 180 pounds.

5

Now I am not sad. I have something good to eat. Thank you.

8

1

Look, I will make this for you. Will you like it?

6

I want something to eat. I want something good to eat.

3

Little one, why do you
look sad?

2

Yes, that is good. I will
like that.

7

Come here. I will make you
something to eat.
I will make you something good
to eat.

4

Sit here. It will not take
too long. You will have something to eat.

5

I will get that, too.
They cook good things to eat.
I like to eat here.

8

BOOK 11

Let's Go Out

1

We can go here to eat.
They will have something good
to eat.

6

I like to go out to eat.

3

Let's do something new. Let's
go out to eat.

2

I will get this. What will
you get?

7

Let's put on something pretty.
I like to look good to go out.

4

Look how good we look! Let's
go now.

5

Look at me!
You did find my keys. Thank
you. You are a big help.
8

1

Are your keys in here?
I will look in here.
Your keys are not in here.
6

I cannot go out now.
I have to look for my keys.
3

29

Where did I put my keys? I
cannot find my keys.

2

I know where your keys are. I
see your keys. You have your
keys. Look here.

7

Can you help me find my keys?
I do not know where I put
my keys.

4

I will help you look for your
keys. You know I will help.
We will find your keys.

5

Yes, a walk is good. Now I am well. I will not do that again. I will not eat too much again.

8

BOOK 13

I Ate Too Much

1

Well, well, you did eat too much. I cannot get you up. Let me see how I can get you up.

6

Yes, I ate too much. Now I am not well.

3

You do not look well. How much did you eat? Did you eat too much?

2

Now we will get you up. We will get you up to go for a walk. A walk will help you.

7

Let's go for a walk. A walk will help you.

4

Help me get up.
First, I have to get up to go for a walk.

5

Yes, this is funny. You did show me something funny. I think you are funny.

8

BOOK 14

Something Funny

1

Open it and you will see. I think you will like it.

6

Yes, you may show me something funny. I would like to see something funny.

3

33

I want to show you something
funny. May I show you something funny?

2

Well, I will open it.
I may not like it.
I will look and see.

7

Open this.
I think it is funny.

4

You want me to open this?
Is something funny in there?
Did you put something funny in
here?

5

Yes, I will buy the book, and I will laugh. Thank you for your help.

8

BOOK 15

A Book to Read

1

Yes, I think that would be good. I would like to laugh before I go to sleep.

6

Yes, I would like something to read. I would like something funny to read.

3

May I help you find some-thing?

2

You will like this book. Would you like to buy it?

7

I cannot sleep well, so I want something to read before I go to sleep.

4

Look, I can show you a funny book. This is a funny book. It will make you laugh. Do you want to laugh before you go to sleep?

5

I like to see them play ball.
They know how to run and get
the ball in.

8

Book 16

Play Ball

1

Will he get the ball in?
Will he get it in now?

6

Look at him!
He can run fast.
Did you see him run fast?

3

I want to see them play ball.
Let's see them play ball. They
can play ball!

2

Did you see that?
He got the ball in. He did it!
He did it!

7

He can jump up to get the ball.
Did you see him jump up to get
the ball?

4

Look at him run. Look at him
run to get the ball.

5

Thank you for your help. I must go now. I will tell you about work when I see you.

8

BOOK 17

Something to Take to Work

1

Yes, I will take that to work. I will take a cold drink, too.

6

Yes, I will help you. What about some of this?

3

39

I must go to work now. I want
to take something to eat. Can
you help me make something
to take to work?

2

A cold drink is always good.

7

No, I always take that. I do
not want to take that again. I
want something new.

4

What about this? This is always good to take. Would you
like it?

5

Look! Here is the bus. I will get on the bus and ride down-town. Thank you for the help.

8

Book 18

Bus Stop

1

Is it a long ride downtown? Will it take long to get down-town from here?

6

Here is the bus stop. The bus will stop here, and then it will go downtown.

3

I want to go downtown. I want
to get on the bus that goes
downtown. Where is the
bus stop?

2

It will not take too long. The
bus will be here soon, and it
will not take too long to
get downtown.

7

Will the bus come soon? Will
it stop here soon?

4

Yes, the bus will stop here
soon. It will not take too long
for the bus to come.

5

BOOK 19

Tell Me about It

1

That will be good. Please tell
him I said hello.

8

He said for me to tell you
"Hello." He said that he would
see you soon.

6

What's up, Kim?
Please tell me who you saw.

3

Hello Pat. I must tell you who
I saw.

2

Yes, I will see him soon. He
will call me soon, and then we
will go out to eat.

7

I went to get a cold drink, and
I saw Sam there.

4

You saw Sam there? Please
tell me all about it. Tell me
what he said. Did he say something about me?

5

That Is Pretty

Too Much Work

Nothing Is Clean

51

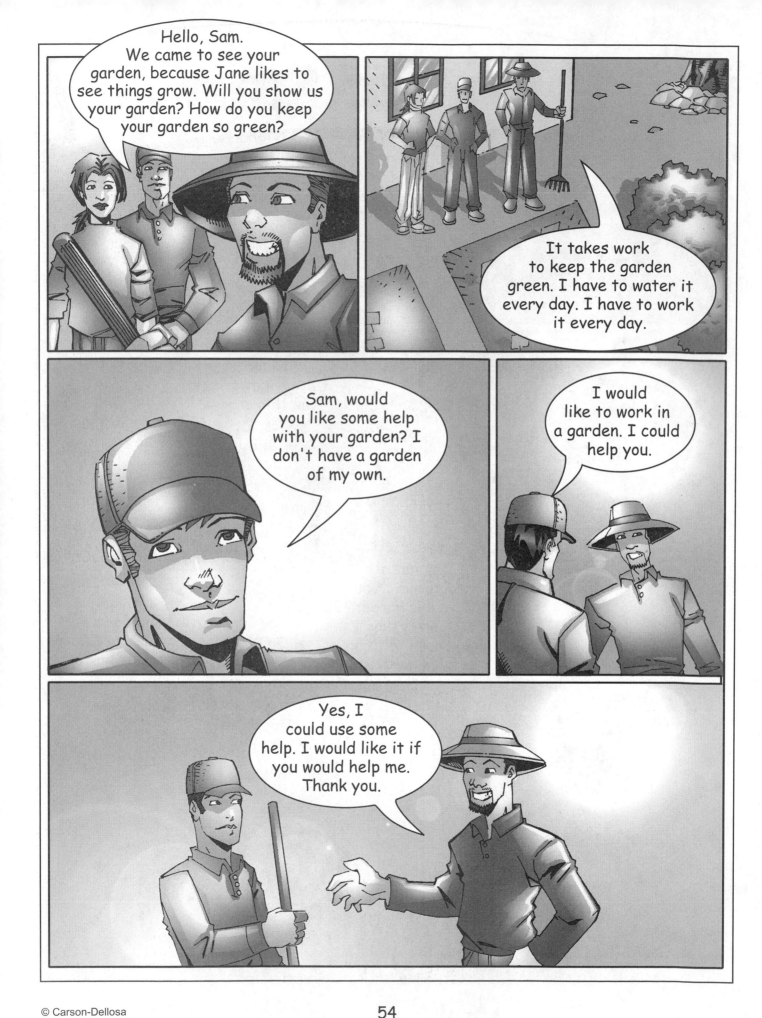

How to Start

Kim, you are sitting there like you don't know what to do. What are you thinking about?

I want to draw, but I don't know how to start.

You could pick a color and just start to draw anything.

Give me your box of colors, and I will help you pick one.

Let's Go Somewhere

Going Away

I am going away today. I am going away to see an old man I know. When I was small, about five or six, I would go to see him. He was very kind to me.

Do you write to him or call him to find out how he is doing?

Yes, I write to him. That is how I know that he got hurt. I want to see him and help him if I can. That is the best thing that I can do.

It Is So Good

Getting a Job

Kim, how do I look? Today I am going to see a man about a job. I want to look good when I go there.

Jack, I think you look just right. What kind of job is it that you will try to get.

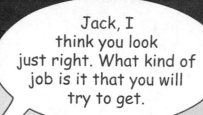

It is a small job at the bookstore. I will put out the books so that everyone can see them and buy them. The pay is good, so I can buy something that I need.

I wish you well. I know that you will do a good job. I will come by the bookstore today to see if you get the job.

65

8

1

6

3

2   7

- -

4   5

Comprehension Questions

Book 1

What is the boy watching on TV?
What do you like to watch on TV?
Why do you like it?

Book 2

What is this story about?
Why do they want to know what is in the box?
Why do you think the cake is in the box?

Book 3

What do they want to play?
What were they looking for?
What do you think they will do next?

Book 4

Where is the lady?
Why does she have a list?
What is she going to buy?
How will she pay?

Book 5

Which one will the man buy?
Why won't he buy the first two?
When you shop, whom do you go shopping with?
How do you find things to fit you?

Book 6

Why does he like the last car?
Should he buy it just because it looks good?
What else should he think about before buying the car?

Book 7

Where did he go in his new car? Why?
What does his friend think about the car?
If you could get a new car, what kind would it be?

Book 8

What is this story about?
Why does she want her hair cut?
Who cuts her hair?
What does her friend think about her haircut?
Where do you go to get your hair cut?

Book 9

Where might he be that he would have to answer these questions?
Have you ever had to answer these kinds of questions? Where were you?
Can you fill out the form on the back of the book?

Book 10

What is the kid's problem?
Who is helping?
Why does the kid feel better at the end of the story?

Book 11

Where did they go?
Why did they dress up?
Why did they pick that place?
Where do you like to go for dinner? Why?

Book 12

What is the problem in this story?
Who is helping?
How did they solve the problem?
Do you ever lose things?

Book 13

What is this story about?
Why does the man feel better at the end?
Do you think he will learn a lesson, or will he do it again?
How do you feel when you eat way too much?

Book 14

What is the surprise in this story?
Has anyone ever played a trick on you?
What was it? How did you feel about it?
How did the surprise in this story work?

Book 15

Why does the lady want a book?
What kind of book does she want?
What do you think she will do tonight?

Book 16

What is this story about?
How do these people feel about watching the game?
Do you think they can play the game? Why?
What sports do you play?

Book 17

Why does he want help?
Why does he want something new?
Where is he going?
If you were making his lunch, what would you make?

Book 18

What is this story about?
Where does it take place?
Why does this person have so many questions?
Do you ever ride the bus? What is it like?

Book 19

How often do you think these girls talk on the telephone?
Who is Sam?
Why are they talking about him?
Who do you talk to on the telephone?

Book 20

Where does this story take place?
Why didn't she let the other lady help her?
Why did she decide to buy two?
What do you think she will do with them?

Book 21

What is this story about?
Why will Sam help out?
What do they have to do first?
What will they get when the work is done?
What do you think they will do after work?

Book 22

What is the problem in the story?
Where does he have to go to fix the problem?
While he is there, what else does he do?
Where do you think Sam and Jane will go?

Book 23

Why couldn't he see Jane?
Where did Jane go?
What should Jane have done before she went away?
What are they going to do now?

Book 24

What is this story about?
Why did they go visit Sam?
What did Sam tell them?
What will Jane do?
How do you think Sam feels about it?

Book 25

What is Kim's problem?
Why isn't the crayon box full?
What is Kim going to do?
How do you think it will turn out?
If you were going to draw, what would you draw?

Book 26

What are the girls going to do?
Why are they going to call Jane?
Where did the three of them go once before?
Where do you think they should go?

Book 27

What is this story about?
What happened to the old man?
How do the wheels make things easier?
How does his friend want to help?

Book 28

How did Sam get there?
What will he have for a snack?
How do the people feel about Sam's visit?

Book 29

What is the story about?
Where are they hiding the presents?
Why did Jack have to go to the store?
What did everyone do when Kate got there?

Book 30

Why is Jack concerned about his appearance?
How does Kim encourage him?
Does he get the job? What is the job?
How does he feel about the job?

Dolch Word List

the	then	its	help	start	pull
to	little	ride	make	black	cut
and	down	into	going	white	kind
he	do	just	sleep	ten	both
a	can	blue	brown	does	sit
I	could	red	yellow	bring	which
you	when	from	five	goes	fall
it	did	good	six	write	carry
of	what	any	walk	always	small
in	so	about	two	drink	under
was	see	around	or	once	read
said	not	want	before	soon	why
his	were	don't	eat	made	own
that	get	how	again	run	found
she	them	know	play	gave	wash
for	like	right	who	open	show
on	one	put	been	has	hot
they	this	got	may	find	because
but	my	take	stop	only	far
had	would	where	off	us	live
at	me	every	never	three	draw
him	will	pretty	seven	our	clean
with	yes	jump	eight	better	grow
up	big	green	cold	hold	best
all	went	four	today	buy	on
look	are	away	fly	funny	these
is	come	old	myself	warm	sing
her	if	by	round	ate	together
there	now	their	tell	full	please
some	long	here	much	those	thank
out	no	saw	keep	done	wish
as	came	call	give	use	many
be	ask	after	work	fast	shall
have	very	well	first	say	laugh
go	an	think	try	light	too
we	over	ran	new	pick	
am	your	let	must	hurt	

73

© Caroon Dollooa

what	is	this
do	no	too
you	not	little
see	cake	take
I	where	that
a	here	off
TV	can	try
on	bat	big
man	milk	good
ball	bread	looking
hit	fruit	like
box	money	want
in	look	to
the	at	it

buy	long	of
one	cut	birth
am	your	age
me	sit	height
have	make	feet
come	pretty	inches
new	now	weight
did	got	pounds ad-
yes	looks	dress
for	will	hill
ride	name	street
get	Dan	telephone
when	Hale	number
hair	date	why

sad	cannot	funny
something	find	may
eat	help	would
that	know	open
thank	are	think
let's	well	read
out	much	sleep
put	age	laugh
how	walk	before
we	up	so
they	first	book
cook	again	them
things	let	play
keys	show	he

run	downtown	say
fast	goes	what's
him	stop	all
jump	from	Sam
work	then	found
must	soon	by
always	hello	books
about	Pat	or
some	Kim	comes
cold	who	two
drink	saw	colors
tell	please	blue
again	there	green
bus	said	which

should	nothing	her
both	clean	was
today	wash	just
pay	going	with
but	laundromat	don't
together	anything	she
because	water	went
use	hot	could
carry	things	does
better	warm	live
these	Jane	around
those	doing	lives
many	after	were
done	home	looked

call	likes	yellow
wish	sitting	brown
had	thinking	black
garden	draw	white
grow	start	right
every	pick	anywhere
day	give	somewhere
has	full	far
been	eight	away
his	only	ask
came	seven	us
keep	gave	fun
takes	orange	three
own	red	shall

once	into	sing
hurt	pull	their
kind	an	Jack
old	our	ten
small	from	everything
five	fly	everyone
six	as	birthday
very	bring	surprise
write	round	coming
best	on	job
light	plate	bookstore
four	Mr. Jake	need
its	ran	
wheels	under	